Copyright © 2025 Sarita Talwai, Nidhi Byaravalli

All rights reserved.

This book or any portion thereof may not be reproduced or used in any manner whatsoever without the express written permission of the respective writer of the respective content except for the use of brief quotations in a book review.

The writer of the respective work holds sole responsibility for the originality of the content and IndiePress is not responsible in any way whatsoever.

Printed in India

ISBN: 978-93-6045-778-5

First Printing, 2025

IndiePress

A division of Nasadiya Technologies Private Ltd.

Koramangala, Bangalore

Karnataka-560029

http://indiepress.in/

Book Cover designed by Nidhi Byaravalli

Publishing Consultant - Souvik Bhattacharjee

To family and friends

"Haiku is not a shriek, a howl, a sigh, or a yawn; rather, it is the deep breath of life."

Santōka Taneda

Indian summer
freshly pounded turmeric
travels through the town

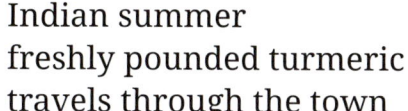

oh elephant calf
how you transform us again
into mushy moms

hate speech on TV
a weapon exchanges hands
in a distant town

end of a visit
I leave my love behind
in casseroles

poet at the desk
dips into a thesaurus
to find his feelings

spring
enters the picture
on a leaf

evening walk
an abandoned hopscotch grid
beckons me

scorching summer noon
a young tree trying to rest
in its own shadow

returning from work
father kicks a phantom ball
into the darkness

a dried rosebud
inside a secondhand book
another story

migratory bird
seeks a resident pigeon
who knows the city

teenage alien
influenced by the earthlings
demands his own space

holiday dinner
a simple curry garnished
with opinions

at the therapist
opaque ink blot test reveals
a flicker of light

those poor daisies
repeatedly falling prey
to confused lovers

exhausted options
the weary mom surrenders
to instant noodles

thunder in the sky
elephants in a mud bath
the earth rejoices

when I don't chase words
I find them standing in line
waiting to be used

betrayed by the clouds
sunflowers turn to each other
for affirmation

stuffed toys all lined up
quiet anticipation
just before bedtime

a rainy morning
the blue crayon in the box
becoming shorter

who will tell the weeds
that they are not flowers
how will they know?

bonsai tree
near the window
looking out

relentless ivy
no need of a cavalry
to conquer the fort

sentient robot
attached to its engineer
it's a trauma bond

stagnant pond tickled
released by the dragonfly
some trapped laughter

faded cricket stumps
peering through the mossy walls
that border childhood

display in the shop
of elephants holding tails
I call my mother

armchair activist
enraged that his daily rage
has no audience

weekly video call
a mother's eye noticing
the pile of laundry

toddler at lunchtime
hypnotised by a cartoon
eats a balanced meal

moves in the kitchen
mustard seeds and curry leaves
dance to their own beat

two bottles of wine
the karaoke machine
wishes we would stop

sharp slats in my blinds
slicing the nearby high-rise
to bite-size pieces

the hardy poet
writes a tentative poem
on an unpaid bill

edge of the jungle
the elephant corridor
now has traffic lights

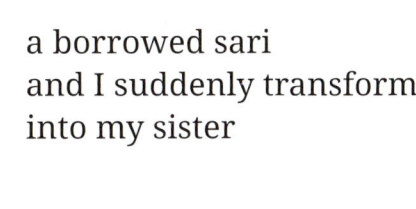

a borrowed sari
and I suddenly transform
into my sister

train in the tunnel
some thankful for the darkness
some await the light

and what is anger
but long standing sadness
homeless and orphaned

inside the classroom
the boy remembers the days
before he could write

through the train window
Van Gogh's sunflowers now
a streak of yellow

lonely amidst friends
longs for his TV dinner
and his solitude

book of quotes
i read aloud
in my father's voice

glorious wildflower
in a crack in the pavement
how I notice you

alone at the table
the steam from the hot rice
calligraphs a name

squeak of the old swing
smothers the cacophony
of pending homework

the tawny eagle
adjusting to city life
lines nest with plastic

extreme conditions
robot in the lab makes friends
with the table fan

seize the day they say
but what if we just allow
the day to seize us

hungry bookends
stretching their appetite
to all genres

to the steady ant
on the rim of a tea cup
a vast horizon

at the optician
figuring out if my face
is oval or round

all our profound thoughts
summarily discarded
poetry workshop

summer holidays
swimming pool full of children
with amnesia

the gentle giant
allows the mahout to dream
of becoming king

if you gaze for long
every cloud in the sky starts
to tell a story

petri dish prison
mutinous bacteria
multiply fiercely

at the airport lounge
furrows on the mother's face
match those on the son's

Schrödinger's salmon
is your arduous journey
worthless or fruitful?

hide-and-seek
hoping to be not found then
yearning to be found

last cup of the set
I sip away a childhood
very carefully

too much religion
and too little compassion
the gods are weary

Sarita Talwai is a Bangalore-based counsellor, who especially likes to work with children and parents. She is also a Gallup Strengths coach. As a facilitator at Bangalore Writers Workshop she has conducted creative writing workshops for children. She is the ambitious owner of a stack of unread books and an incomplete manuscript.
Her friends though, insist that she is mostly a curious bystander, and she is inclined to agree with them. She spends her free time reading poetry and attempting to write the perfect haiku.

Nidhi B.R. is an architect and designer who believes that good design has the power to infuse joy into everyday life. With a minimalist approach and a sharp eye for detail, he creates functional yet thought-provoking works that blend simplicity with depth.
His illustrations go beyond the obvious, inviting curiosity and exploration while revealing hidden layers of meaning. When not designing, he finds solace in sketching and immersing himself in nature, drawing endless inspiration from its quiet elegance.

We would like to thank the following people for the various kinds of help and support they have given us over the years.
Aaditya Talwai, Ajita Panshikar, Bhumika Anand, Clifferd D'mello, Nisha Shetty, Prabha Mallesh Athihalli, Ravi Talwai, Ravikumar Byaravalli, Saachi Talwai, Saraswathi Kujugodu, buddies and mentors from DMPS, SSSLSVK_Alike, Mahesh PUC, RVCA and DM_IISc.

A poetic sensibility can be honed, but Sarita is one of the few lucky ones who has always known how to appreciate the world around us replete as it is with simple joys and profound insights. In this book you will enjoy this flavour of her poetics and delight in her great love for language.

Nidhi's charming illustrations harken back to the grand masters of the Haiku tradition, particularly Issa, who illustrated his syllables.

Together, Sarita and Nidhi present the reader with an enchanting postcard on each page.

Bhumika Anand
Founder and Director
Bangalore Writers Workshop (BWW)

IndiePress

The best route your story can take.
To publish your own book, contact us.
We publish poetry collections, short story collections,
novellas and novels.

contact@http://indiepress.in/
Instagram- indie_press

We would love to hear from you

Instagram
everyday_haiku_book

mail
talwai_s@yahoo.co.in
akeytocreate@gmail.com